COPYRIGHT © 2025 PAST TO PRESENT PUBLISHING LLC

PUBLISHED BY PAST TO PRESENT PUBLISHING LLC

ALL RIGHTS RESERVED.

THIS BOOK MAY NOT BE COPIED, REPRODUCED, STORED IN A RETRIEVAL SYSTEM, OR TRANSMITTED IN ANY FORM OR BY ANY MEANS INCLUDING ELECTRONIC, MECHANICAL, PHOTOCOPYING, RECORDING, OR OTHERWISE, WITHOUT PRIOR WRITTEN PERMISSION FROM THE PUBLISHER, EXCEPT FOR BRIEF QUOTATIONS USED IN REVIEWS, ARTICLES, OR EDUCATIONAL PURPOSES AS PERMITTED UNDER U.S. COPYRIGHT LAW.

THIS BOOK IS INTENDED TO PROVIDE EDUCATIONAL AND HISTORICAL INFORMATION ON THE SUBJECT MATTER COVERED. THE AUTHOR AND PUBLISHER HAVE MADE EVERY EFFORT TO ENSURE ACCURACY BUT THEY MAKE NO REPRESENTATIONS OR WARRANTIES REGARDING THE COMPLETENESS OR APPLICABILITY OF THE CONTENT. NEITHER THE PUBLISHER, THE AUTHOR, NOR ANY OTHER CONTRIBUTORS TO THIS BOOK SHALL BE LIABLE FOR ANY DIRECT, INDIRECT, INCIDENTAL, CONSEQUENTIAL, OR SPECIAL DAMAGES ARISING FROM THE USE OR INTERPRETATION OF THIS MATERIAL. READERS ARE ENCOURAGED TO CONDUCT THEIR OWN RESEARCH AND CONSULT PROFESSIONALS FOR SPECIFIC ADVICE.

WRITTEN AND ILLUSTRATED BY LARRY CLINKSCALES JR

PRINTED IN THE UNITED STATES OF AMERICA.
ISBN: 979-8-9924926-1-3

FOR PERMISSIONS, INQUIRIES, OR BULK ORDERS, CONTACT:
PAST TO PRESENT PUBLISHING LLC
ADDRESS: 1515 MOCKINGBIRD LN SUITE 420, CHARLOTTE, NC 28209
PHONE NUMBER: (980) 428-6062
EMAIL: PASTTOPRESENTPUBLISHING@GMAIL.COM

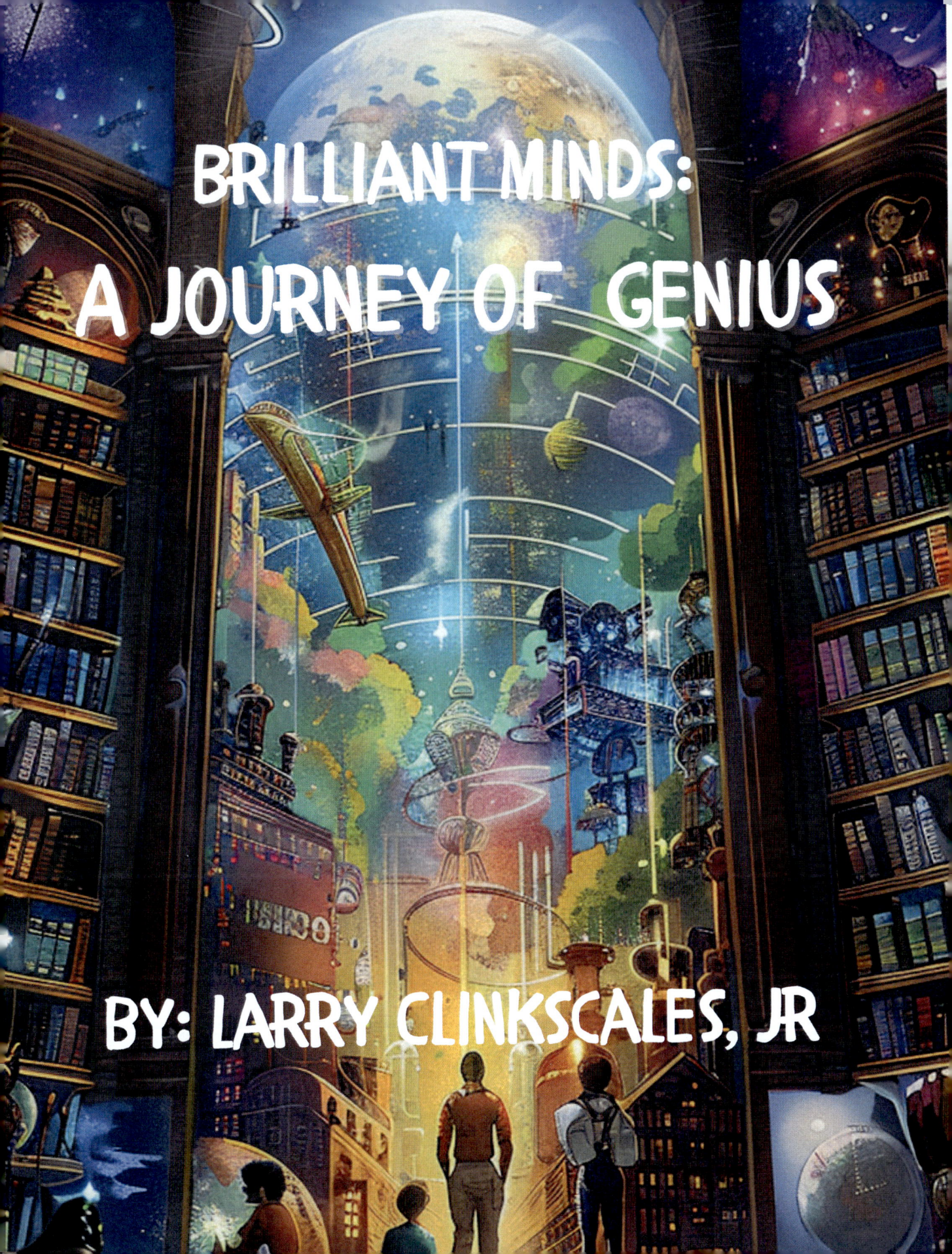

Dedication:
To my sons Jeremiah and Trey, who move me to share history that inspires!

BRILLIANT MINDS: A JOURNEY OF GENIUS VOL 1

IN A WORLD OF WONDER AND DELIGHT
WHERE INNOVATION FILLED THE AIR,
LIVED INVENTORS WITH MINDS SO BRIGHT
WHO CRAFTED THINGS SO RARE.

IMAGINE MAKING THINGS SO NEAT;
CREATIONS THAT SPARKLE AND SHINE.
HERE'S TO THE GENIUS OF THE MAKERS
WHOSE IDEAS ARE OH-SO-FINE!

LEWIS LATIMER

CARBON FILAMENT LIGHT BULB

ON A DARK NIGHT
LEWIS LATIMER PONDERED
HOW TO MAKE THE LIGHT BULB STRONGER.
HE MADE ONE SHINE, FOR A LONG TIME
HIS INVENTION LEFT A TRAIL OF LIGHT.
WITH PATENTS HE FILED
HE SPREAD HIS CHEER
SINCE HE MADE MORE ELECTRIC LIGHTS APPEAR!

PHILIP B. DOWNING

MODERN MAILBOX

IN TIMES OF LETTERS INKED JUST RIGHT
PHILIP'S IDEA STOOD UPRIGHT.
THROUGH THE MAILBOX'S DOORWAY
MAIL TOOK FLIGHT
CARRYING OUR WORDS
DAY AND NIGHT.

LONNIE JOHNSON

SUPER SOAKER

Beneath the summer sun
Hot as can be
Lonnie Johnson's invention
Fired a stream.
His Super Soaker was a child's delight
That made regular play
A splish-splash fight!

ALFRED L. CRALLE

ICE CREAM SCOOP

IN THE LAND OF ICE CREAM DREAMS SO SWEET
MR. CRALLE'S IDEA WAS OH SO NEAT.
WITH CURVES THAT SWIRL
AND A DESIGN SO FINE
IT SERVES UP JOY
ONE SCOOP AT A TIME!

GRANVILLE WOODS

MULTIPLEX RAILWAY TELEGRAPH

WITH THE TELEGRAPH'S MAGIC
AND A THOUGHT SO GRAND
GRANVILLE'S USE OF A MAGNET
WAS A FASTER PLAN.
THE TWO TOGETHER
IN A SWIFT DISPLAY
HELP TRAINS SEND MESSAGES
IN A VERY QUICK WAY.

MARIE VAN BRITTAN BROWN

HOME SECURITY SYSTEM

AS NIGHT STARS TWINKLED
FAMILIES SLEPT IN PLACE.
MARIE THOUGHT OF SAFETY
AND SECURING HER SPACE.
ONE QUIET NIGHT SHE DESIGNED
A SECURITY SYSTEM
THE FIRST OF ITS KIND.

GEORGE WASHINGTON CARVER

AGRICULTURAL SCIENTIST

GEORGE WASHINGTON CARVER
THE PLANT DOCTOR WAS HE.
HE MADE PLASTIC OUT OF SOYBEANS
A REAL GENIUS YOU SEE.
CROP ROTATION, ANOTHER PRACTICE
BECAME ESSENTIAL TO EMBRACE.
CARVER'S INFLUENCE ON FARMING
A SAVING GRACE.

ALICE H. PARKER

GAS HEATING FURNACE

ON COLD WINTER DAYS WITH A NIPPY BITE
ALICE'S IDEA HEATS JUST RIGHT.
TO WARM OUR HOMES
WHEN SNOW FALLS
SHE INVENTED A FURNACE
TO COMFORT US ALL.

CHARLES R. DREW

BLOOD BANKING PROCESS

Charles Drew worked
with science and care.
His blood banking process
saved lives everywhere.
He separated plasma from blood
and stored it so well
the procedure became standard
for medical personnel.

GARRETT MORGAN

GAS MASK

WHEN SMOKE AND FUMES FILLED THE AIR
GARRETT MADE A MASK
THAT KEPT HIM PREPARED.
THE MASKS, USED BY HEROES
KEPT THEM SAFE
AS THEY BRAVELY FOUGHT FIRES
WITH DANGEROUS BLAZE.

DR. THOMAS MENSAH

FIBER OPTICS INNOVATION

When the internet started
Things were slow
Dr. Mensah's vision stole the show.
Lightning-speed cables
At such a fast pace
Connecting us all in a digital space!

ISAAC R. JOHNSON

BICYCLE FRAME

ISAAC LOVED BIKES
WHEELS SPINNING WITH SPEED.
HE MADE A STRONG FRAME
A MARVEL TO SEE.
STURDY AND TRUE
WE RIDE SO FREE
BICYCLE ADVENTURES FOR YOU AND ME!

ALEXANDER MILES

AUTOMATIC ELEVATOR DOORS

IN TALL BUILDINGS
WHERE ELEVATORS ROSE
THE DOORS WERE MANUAL
TO OPEN AND CLOSE.
ALEXANDER'S CREATION
MADE IT SO SMOOTH
FOR ELEVATOR DOORS TO REALLY MOVE.

WE HOPE THESE INVENTIONS
TRULY INSPIRE YOU
TO DREAM AND DISCOVER, OR MAKE
SOMETHING LIKE NEW.

THESE INVENTORS, JUST A FEW
OF SO MANY MORE
WHOSE CREATIONS MADE HISTORY
NOW GO AND EXPLORE!

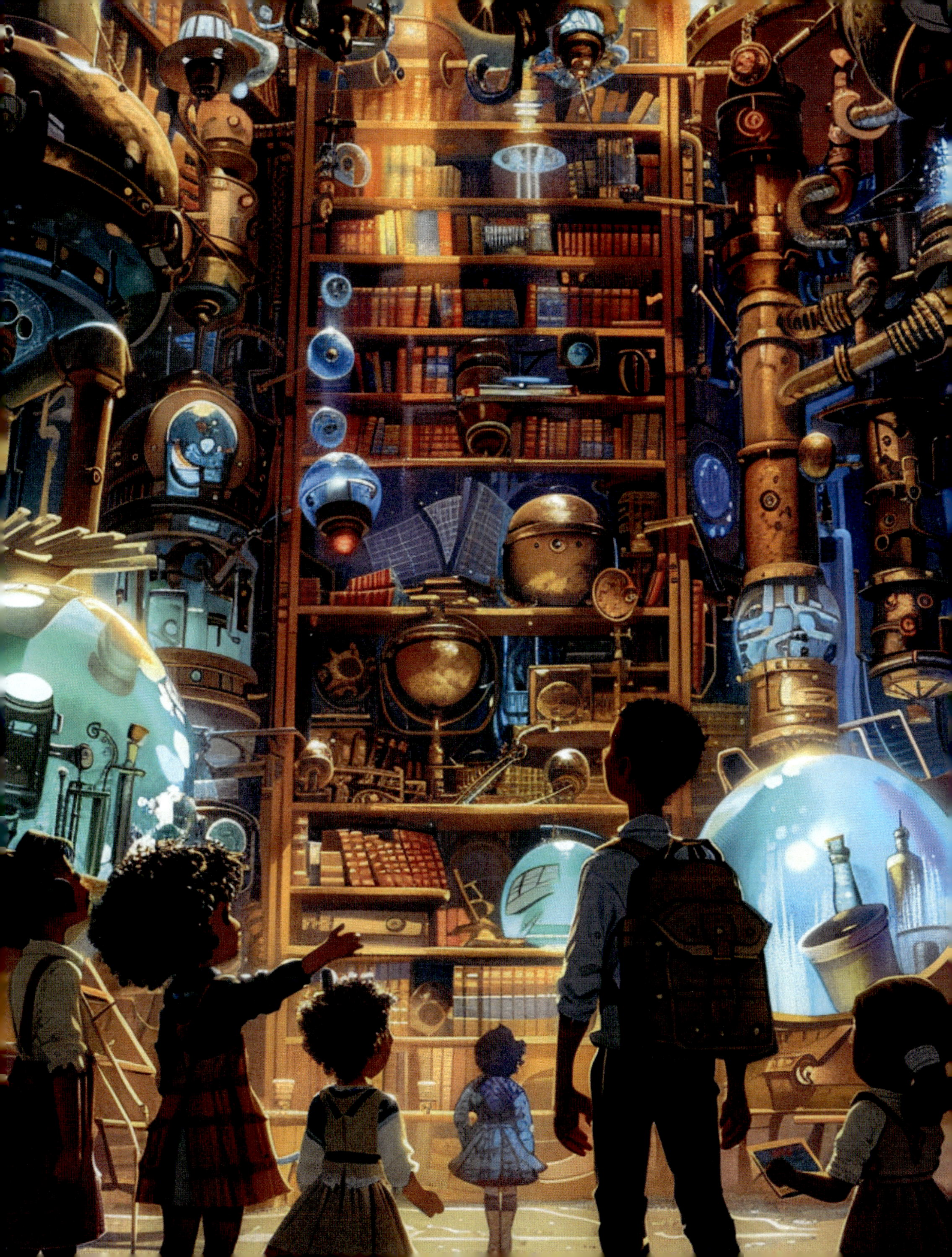

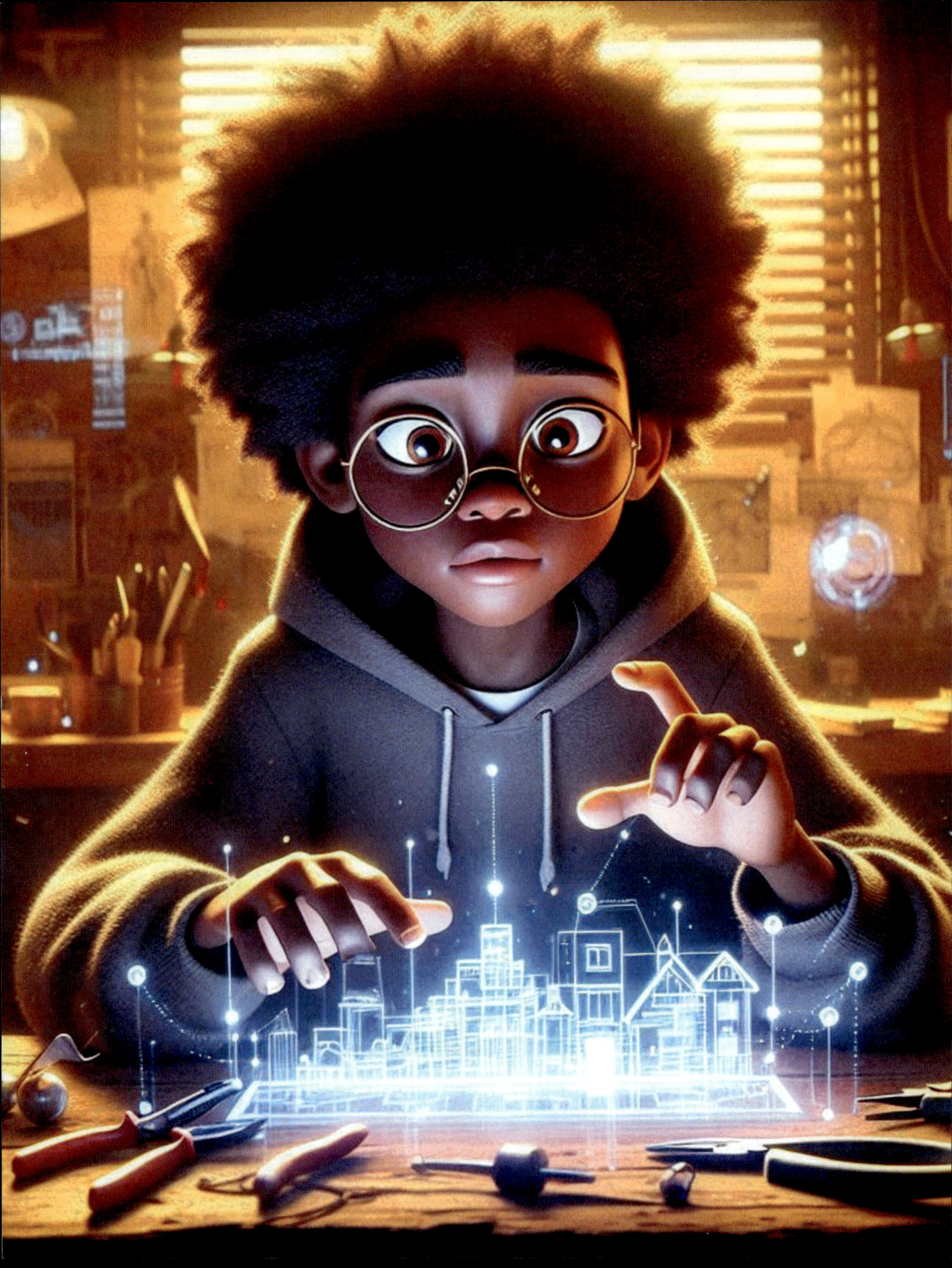

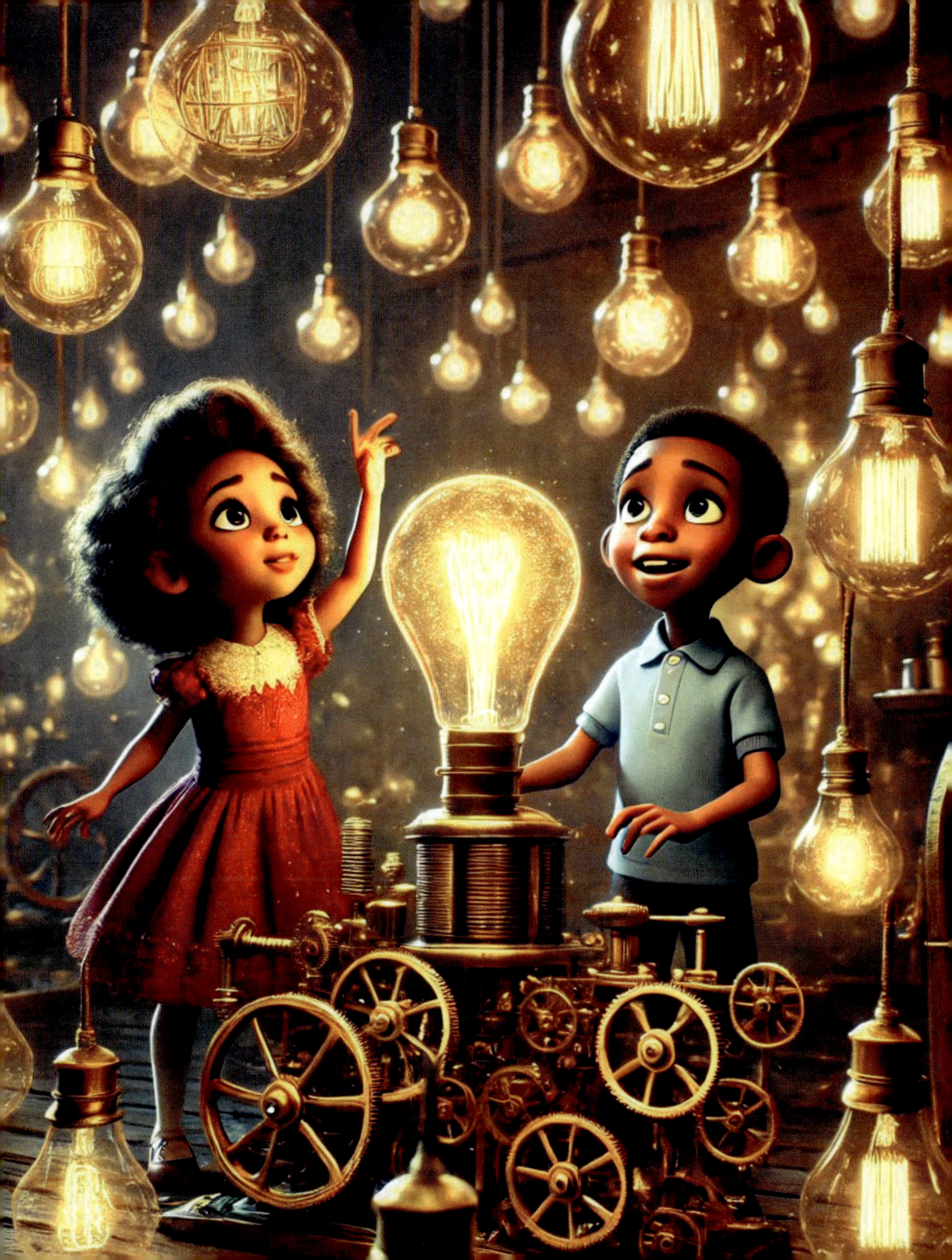

ACKNOWLEGMENTS

This book is a dream realized that would not have been possible without the love and support of those closest to me.

To my wife, Eboni, thank you for being my rock, my encourager, and a constant support throughout this journey. Your help and belief in me encouraged me to keep going, and helped make this possible.

To my family and friends, your willingness to listen to my thoughts, discoveries, challenges, and sharing new ideas, means more than words can express.

Finally, to you the reader, thank you for reading this book. I hope these stories inspire you to dream, explore, and help to unlock your own inner genius.

ABOUT THE AUTHOR

LARRY CLINKSCALES HAS A PASSION FOR WRITING STORIES THAT BEGAN AS A HOBBY OF FILLING NOTEBOOKS WITH IMAGINATIVE TALES. THIS HOBBY LATER GREW INTO A MISSION TO SHARE LESSER-KNOWN STORIES IN BLACK HISTORY WITH YOUNG READERS. WHILE IN SCHOOL GROWING UP, LARRY DID NOT LEARN MUCH ABOUT THE SIGNIFICANT CONTRIBUTIONS OF AFRICAN AMERICANS. THIS FUELED HIS DESIRE FOR EVERY CHILD, REGARDLESS OF RACE, TO LEARN THIS REMARKABLE HISTORY.

LARRY HOPES THAT HIS STORIES WILL HELP BUILD CHILDREN'S CONFIDENCE, AND INSPIRE THEM TO CHASE THEIR DREAMS NO MATTER THE CIRCUMSTANCE.

LARRY IS ORIGINALLY FROM ANDERSON, SC, AND IS A GRADUATE OF TUSKEGEE UNIVERSITY. HE LIVES IN CHARLOTTE, NC WITH HIS WIFE AND TWO SONS.

HENRY SAMPSON

GAMMA ELECTRIC CELL CO-CREATOR

With lots of scientists
reaching for the skies
meet Henry T. Sampson
a really smart guy.
These gamma cells unlocked
wonders for outer space
propelling satellites and rockets
advancing the race.

Made in the USA
Monee, IL
17 February 2025